CORRECTION SYMBOLS

Ab	17	Improper abbreviation
Ad	3	Improper use of adjective or adverb
Agr	8	Error in agreement
Appr	42	Inappropriate level of diction
Awk	14	Awkward construction
Ca	2	Faulty pronoun case
Comp	13	Faulty or incomplete comparison
CS	7	Comma splice
Dgl	12	Dangling modifiers
Dir	41	Indirectness, redundancy, weakening repetition
Emp	36	Lack of needed emphasis
End P	19	Faulty end punctuation
Ex	40	Inexact word
Frag	6	Unacceptable sentence fragment
FS	7	Fused (run-together) sentence
Glos	43	Check glossary
Gr	1-5	Faulty grammar
Int P	20-24	Faulty internal punctuation
Log	33	Faulty logic
Mis Pt	11	Misplaced part
MS	15	Improper manuscript form
Nos	16	Error in use of numbers
Om	13	Careless omission, incomplete construction
P	19-30	Error in punctuation
¶ Coh	32c-d	Paragraph lacks coherence
¶ Con	32h	Paragraph lacks consistent tone
¶ Dev	32e-g	Paragraph is poorly or inadequately developed
¶ Un	32a-b	Paragraph lacks unity
||	35	Faulty parellelism
Plan	31	Paper is poorly planned
Q	25	Faulty punctuation of quoted material
Ref	9	Faulty pronoun reference
S	6-14	Poor sentence structure
Sp	44	Error in spelling
Sub	34	Poor subordination
Syl	18	Improper division of word
T	5	Wrong tense of verb
Var	37	Sentence structure lacks variety
Word P	27-30	Faulty word punctuation
X		Obvious error
?		Is this right? Do you mean this?

PROOFREADERS' MARKS

ℓ	Delete	
ℓ	Delete and close up	
⌣	Close up	
#	Insert space	
stet	Let it stand (i.e., the crossed out material above the dots)	
¶	Begin a new paragraph	
no ¶	Run two paragraphs together	
SP	Spell out (e.g., 20 ft)	
tr	Transpose	
lc	Lowercase a Capital letter	
cap	capitalize a lowercase letter	
O /	Correct an error	
2	Superior number	
3	Inferior number	

⌃	Caret (placed within the text to indicate the point at which a marginal addition to be inserted)	
⊙	Period	
⌃	Comma	
:/	Colon	
;/	Semicolon	
'/	Apostrophe or single quotation mark	
"/"	Quotation marks	
?/	Question mark	
!/	Exclamation point	
=	Hyphen	
—M	Dash	
(/)	Parentheses	
[/]	Brackets	

Glenn Leggett

President Emeritus, Grinnell College

C. David Mead

Michigan State University

William Charvat

Late of Ohio State University

With the editorial supervision of

Richard S. Beal

PRENTICE-HALL
HANDBOOK
FOR WRITERS

EIGHTH EDITION

PRENTICE-HALL, INC.,
Englewood Cliffs, N.J.
07632

Library of Congress Cataloging in Publication Data
Main entry under title:

Prentice-Hall handbook for writers.

Eighth ed.: Prentice-Hall handbook for writers/
GLENN LEGGETT, C. DAVID MEAD, WILLIAM CHARVAT.
Includes index.
1. English language—Rhetoric   2. English
language—Grammar—1950-   .   I. Leggett,
Glenn H., (date).
PE1408.P75 1982   808'.042   81-13973
ISBN 0-13-695734-X   AACR2

PRENTICE-HALL HANDBOOK FOR WRITERS
EIGHTH EDITION
LEGGETT, MEAD, CHARVAT, and BEAL

10   9   8   7   6   5   4   3   2

Development editor: Joyce Perkins
Editorial/production supervision by Virginia Rubens
Interior design by Walter Behnke
Cover design by Wanda Lubelska Design
Manufacturing buyer: Ray Keating

ISBN 0-13-695734-X

PRENTICE-HALL INTERNATIONAL, INC., *London*
PRENTICE-HALL OF AUSTRALIA PTY. LIMITED, *Sydney*
PRENTICE-HALL OF CANADA, LTD., *Toronto*
PRENTICE-HALL OF INDIA PRIVATE LIMITED, *New Delhi*
PRENTICE-HALL OF JAPAN, INC., *Tokyo*
PRENTICE-HALL OF SOUTHEAST ASIA PTE. LTD., *Singapore*
WHITEHALL BOOKS LIMITED, WELLINGTON, *New Zealand*